49 Dogs, 36 Cats
& a Platypus

49 Dogs, 36 Cats & a Platypus

Animal Cartoons
Sidney Harris

RUTGERS UNIVERSITY PRESS
New Brunswick, New Jersey, and London

Library of Congress Cataloging-in-Publication Data

Harris, Sidney.
    49 dogs, 36 cats & a platypus / Sidney Harris.
      p.   cm.
    ISBN 0-8135-2743-0 (paper : alk. paper)
    1. Cartooning—Technique. 2. Animals—Carica-
tures and cartoons. I. Title. II. Title: Forty-nine
dogs, thirty-six cats, and a platypus.
    NC1764.8.A54H37   1999
    741.5—dc21   99-26519
                                             CIP

British Cataloging-in-Publication Data for this book is
available from the British Library

Most of the cartoons in this book have been previously
published and copyrighted by the following publica-
tions: *American Scientist, The Chronicle of Higher Edu-
cation, Discover, Fantasy and Science Fiction, Johns
Hopkins Magazine, National Lampoon, Natural History,
The New Yorker, Playboy, Science, Science 85,* and *The
Wall Street Journal.*

Manufactured in the United States of America

49 Dogs, 36 Cats & a Platypus

"SEE — THEY ALWAYS FIND THEIR WAY HOME."

"THERE'S NINETY-NINE ZILLION OF US, AND THEY THINK THEY'RE RUNNING THINGS."

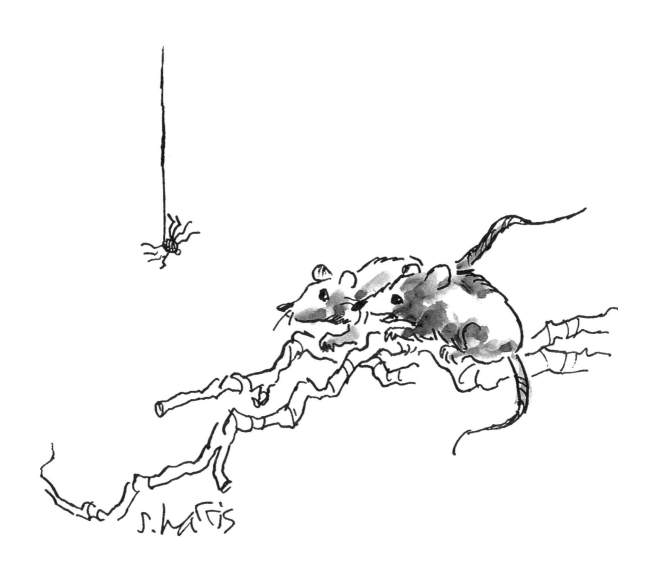

"WE'RE INSECTIVORES. SPIDERS ARE ARACHNIDS. WE DON'T EAT THEM, AND THAT'S THAT."

"...AND YET, I BELIEVE THERE'S A DARK SIDE TO THIS CAREFREE, RURAL LIFE."

"I'VE GOT A MIND NOT TO LEAVE ANYTHING OVER FOR THOSE ANNOYING VULTURES."

"THERE HE GOES FLAUNTING HIS OPPOSABLE THUMB AGAIN."

"THIS IS RUCKUS AND HIS EXTENDED FAMILY."

"GOT A MAP? I'M A HOMING PIGEON, BUT I TOOK A WRONG TURN SOMEWHERE."

"INSTINCT IS NO EXCUSE."

"DIDN'T YOU DO ANYTHING BESIDES WORK ON THAT ANT FARM?"

Type-A personality if I ever saw one—he claims he's now going to swim upstream!

"OUR SPECIALS TODAY ARE BEEF STEW, SALISBURY STEAK... OH, HERE'S ONE YOU'LL LIKE: GARDEN SALAD."

"I'VE BEEN CALLED A LION'S LION. AFTER I FINISH THE CARCASS, I EAT THE HYENAS, AND THEN I EAT THE VULTURES."

"SMELLS ALL RIGHT TO ME, BUT THEN EVERYTHING SMELLS ALL RIGHT TO ME."

"SINCE THAT YOUNG DARWIN FELLOW WAS HERE, THEIR SPECIES CERTAINLY HAS EVOLVED."

"FOR SOMEONE ON THE VERGE OF EXTINCTION, HE LOOKS SURPRISINGLY WELL."

"OF COURSE I'M WORRIED. I HEARD THAT THE LEGS ARE THE FIRST THINGS TO GO."

"LEFTOVERS SOUNDS GOOD."

"I DON'T GET IT — I CAN EAT A GAZILLION PLANKTON, AND I'M STILL HUNGRY."

"BELIEVE ME, SHE'S NO BO-PEEP."

"IF WE COULD JUST FIGURE OUT SOME HIGH-ENERGY DIET, WE WOULDN'T HAVE TO SPEND THE WHOLE DAY EATING."

"MY ADVICE IS KEEP AWAY FROM IT. YOU START WITH CATNIP AND, BEFORE YOU KNOW IT, YOU'RE ON HEROIN."

"ACTUALLY, SEX JUST ISN'T THAT IMPORTANT TO ME."

"I'D LOVE TO GET A DIFFERENT JOB, BUT ALL I KNOW IS BEING A DUNG BEETLE."

"I DON'T CARE IF WE MOSTLY EAT PROTEIN — ON A HOT DAY LIKE THIS I HAVE A CRAVING FOR ICE CREAM."

At least I'm not accused of being envious, lustful, greedy, prideful, gluttonous or wrathful.

J. Harris

"THIS ISN'T MUCH FUN FOR US. EVERY 52 DAYS — BOING! — WE'RE A YEAR OLDER."

"IF ONLY DARWIN COULD HAVE SEEN THIS."

"BELIEVE ME, FOR A PIG, HAVING TO LIVE IN A HOUSE OF STRAW IS NOT THE WORST THING THAT CAN HAPPEN TO YOU."

"WHEN YOU SAID YOU WERE INVITING YOUR COUSIN FOR DINNER..."

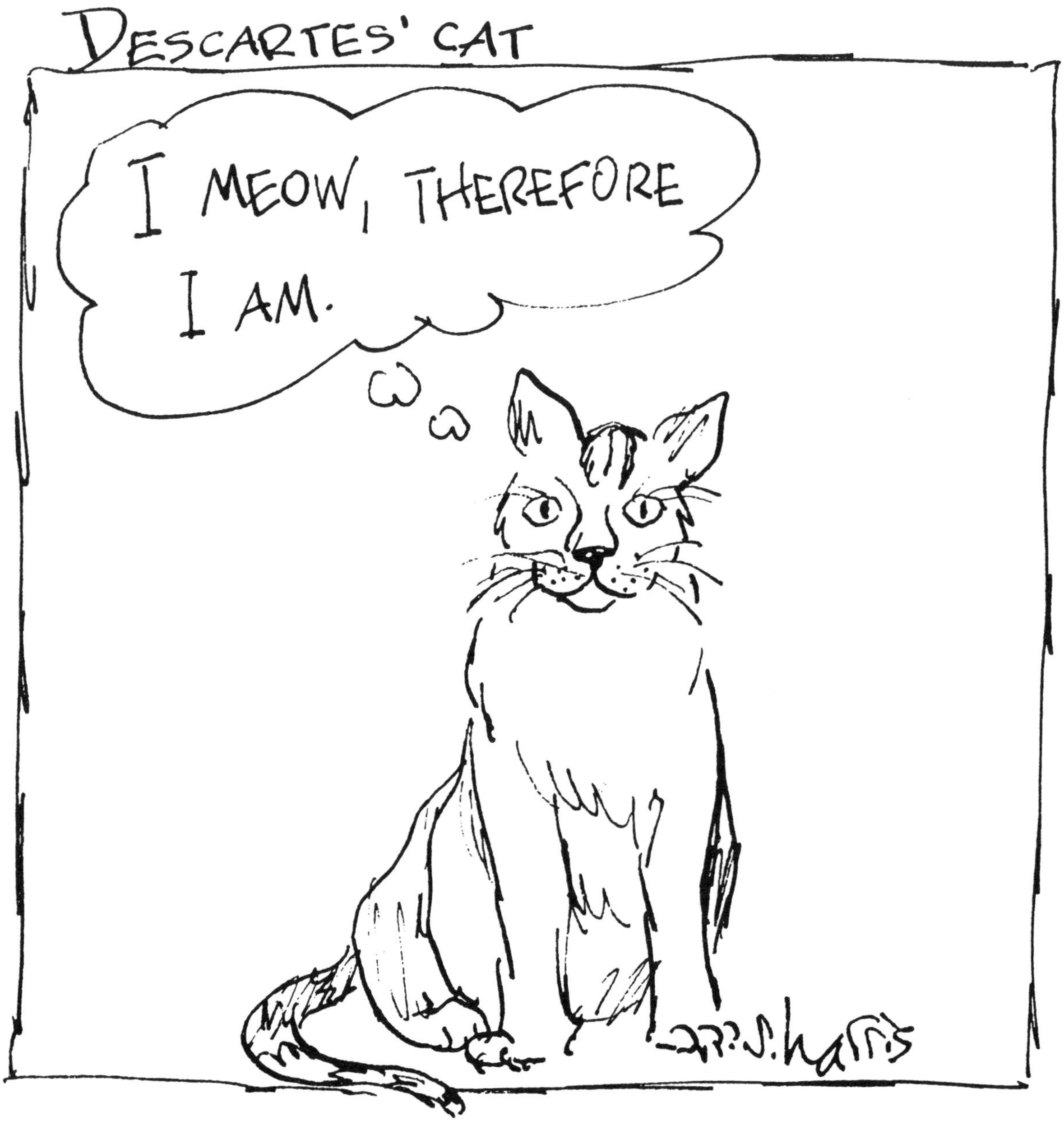
DESCARTES' CAT
I MEOW, THEREFORE I AM.

"I HATE TO BE A WET BLANKET, BUT ONE OF US IS MIGRATING THE WRONG WAY."

"YOU'LL FIND THAT WHEN YOU'RE SEEN ON A MILLION-VOLT ELECTRON MICROSCOPE, YOU REALLY WANT TO LOOK YOUR BEST."

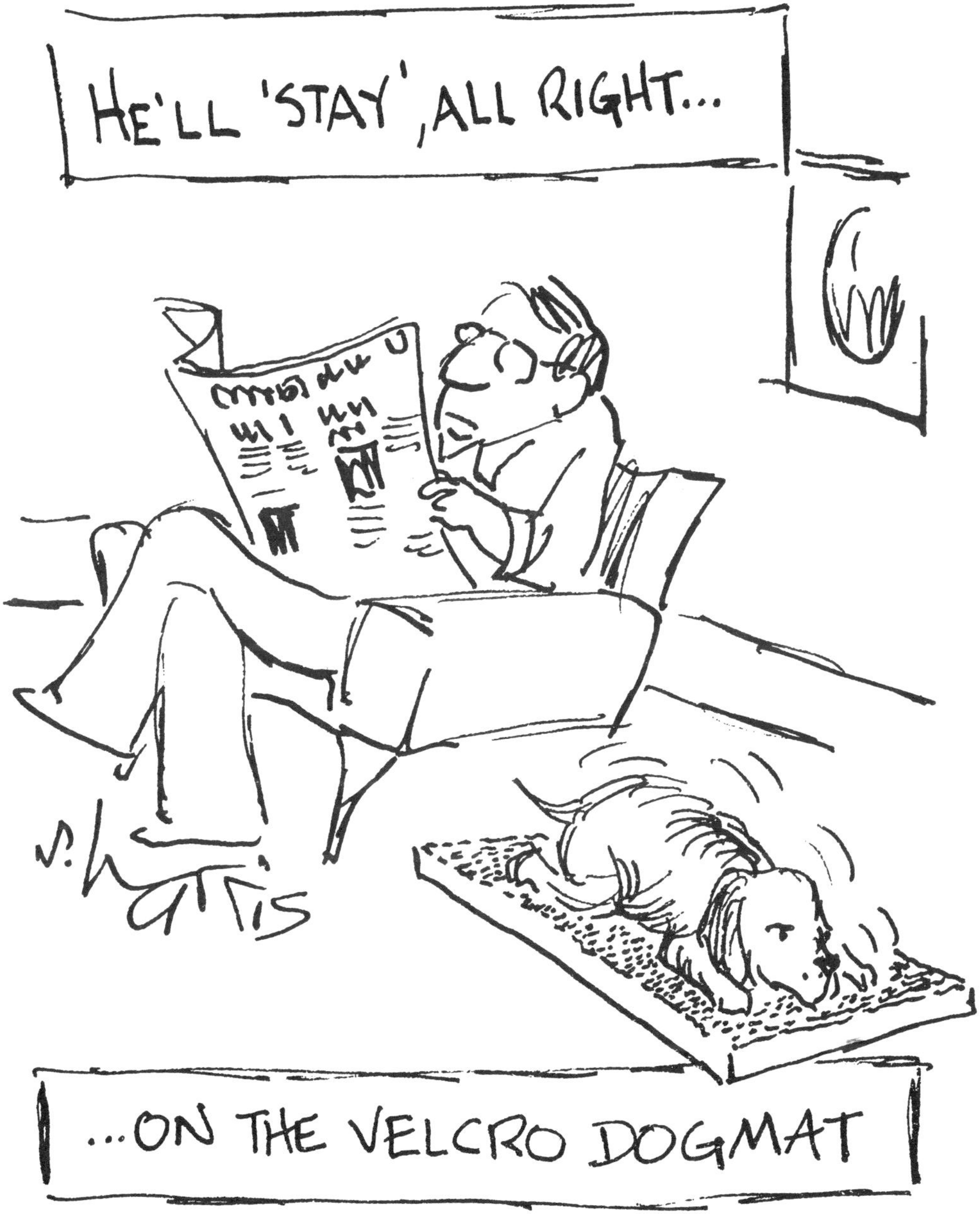
HE'LL 'STAY', ALL RIGHT...
...ON THE VELCRO DOGMAT

"ANTELOPES, ZEBRAS, GIRAFFES — IT CERTAINLY IS A CONSUMER-ORIENTED SOCIETY."

...and we can count to eight. That's more than you can say for them
S. Harris

"THIS YEAR LET'S MIGRATE IN THE OFF-SEASON WHEN TRAFFIC ISN'T SO HEAVY."

"A STAMPEDE? WITH RUNNING?
US? FORGET IT!"

"I EAT THEM MYSELF, AND I CAN ASSURE YOU THAT BEETLES ARE EVEN <u>BETTER</u> THAN ANTS."

"BUT THEN THE WARM WEATHER COMES ALONG, AND YOU REGRET BEING SO DAMN WOOLLY."

"FIRST OF ALL WE WANT OUR NAME CHANGED FROM 'COCKROACH' TO 'COMPANION BEETLE'."

"SINCE I'VE BEEN NEUTERED I HAVE A LOT MORE PLATONIC FRIENDS THAN I USED TO HAVE."

"I SAY WE START EATING NUTS AND BERRIES, AND CLEAN UP OUR IMAGE."

"SURE HE'S CALM — YOU NEVER HEAR OF A WOLF IN SHEPHERD'S CLOTHING."

SHE HUNTS, SHE BRINGS IT BACK, AND MY MANHOOD, THANK GOODNESS, REMAINS INTACT.
S. Harris

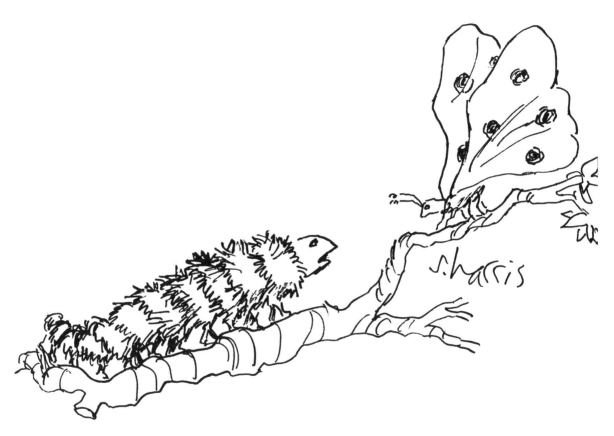

"GREAT DISGUISE, MAX. HOW'D YOU DO IT?"

*How can I think without words?

"I'M THE DOG HE NEVER HAD."

Peace on earth, good will toward crows.
Peace on earth, good will toward frogs.
Peace on earth, good will toward chipmunks.
Peace on earth, good will toward turtles.
Peace on earth, good will toward bugs.
S. Harris

"COULD WE GO IN AHEAD OF YOU? HIS TRANQUILIZER IS WEARING OFF."

"I'VE TOLD YOU TIME AND AGAIN, IF YOU DIDN'T EAT SO FAST, YOU WOULDN'T SWALLOW SO MUCH FLOTSAM."

"I HEARD YOU GUYS ARE REAL FINICKY EATERS."

"I'M PLANNING TO FILE A SEX-DISCRIMINATION COMPLAINT. THEY DIDN'T LET ME RUN WITH THE BULLS IN PAMPLONA."

"IF IT'S TRUE THAT THE WORLD ANT POPULATION IS 10^{15}, THEN IT'S NO WONDER WE NEVER RUN INTO ANYONE WE KNOW."

"YOU'LL JUST HAVE TO _ACCEPT_ THE FACT THAT THEY'RE MORE CONCERNED WITH THEIR FURNITURE THAN WITH YOU."

"WHAT'S ALL THIS PETS' RIGHTS STUFF ADDRESSED TO YOU?"

"A GOOD QUESTION. ACTUALLY I GOT INTO THE BUSINESS WHEN SOME CONSERVATIONISTS UP IN CANADA TAGGED ME WITH A TINY RADIO TRANSMITTER."

"I'M AN AMPHIBIAN ON MY MOTHER'S SIDE AND A REPTILE ON MY FATHER'S SIDE."

"ON THE OTHER HAND, I REALLY DON'T DO THAT MUCH READING."

"MY MAIN FEAR IS THAT WE'LL BECOME EXTINCT BEFORE WE'RE DISCOVERED."

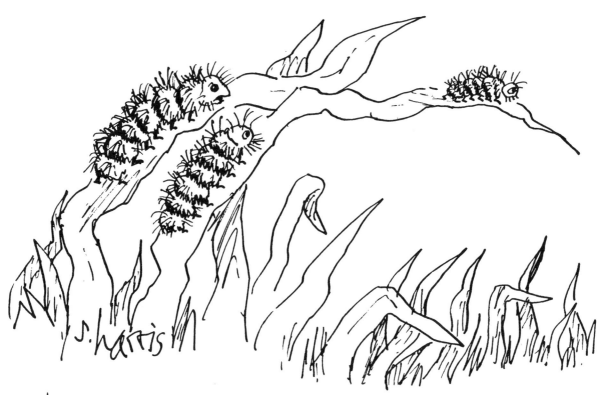

"WHERE DID WE GO WRONG? HE WANTS TO BE AN EXTERMINATOR."

"WITH ANY ENTREE, YOU GET UNLIMITED ACCESS TO THE TROUGH."

"I BELIEVE IT'S TIME WE STOPPED RELYING SO HEAVILY ON INSTINCT."

PROBABILITY

IF YOU HAVE 5 CATS, 4 WILL BE ASLEEP

"ALL IT SAYS IS 'LOYAL AND TRUSTWORTHY FRIEND', BUT THAT'S NOT THE REAL ME."

"IT STARTED WITH THE REMORAS, BUT THEN I PICKED UP A CATFISH, A FEW RAYS, AN EEL, SOME PERCH..."

"BUT WHEN YOU'RE A WART HOG, WARTS ARE WHERE IT'S AT."

"THIS STUFF IS ALL RIGHT, BUT WE PREFER THE FLOTSAM AND JETSAM OF EVERYDAY LIFE."

THE BRAIN-DRAIN HITS THE GOMANGO JUNGLE
It's pretty dull around here since all our best minds have left for the Primate Learning Centers.

"THIS MONTH'S ISSUE IS JUST <u>LOADED</u> WITH THOSE PHEROMONE SCENT-STRIPS."

"ANTHROPOMORPHISM — THAT'S WHERE THE MONEY IS."

Things we rarely hear...

"WE DON'T HAVE ANXIETY—WE CAUSE IT."

"IT MUST BE AN ENTIRELY DIFFERENT SPECIES."

I think I'll give her that enigmatic look that convinces her I have some higher, mysterious power.
S. Harris

"THEY'RE ALWAYS BUSY WITH SOMETHING—THEY INTERACT AND THEY BUILD THINGS—BUT THERE'S NO INDICATION THAT THEY ACTUALLY <u>THINK</u>."

"YOU'RE RIGHT ABOUT HOW HARD IT IS TO TELL US APART. I'M A CROCODILE, BUT FOR YEARS I THOUGHT I WAS AN ALLIGATOR."

How we've evolved — one day we're fetching a stick, the next day we're dealing with that aerodynamic miracle, the frisbee!
s. harris

"YOU'VE HEARD OF THE 'ORIGIN OF THE SPECIES'? — THAT'S US!"

"WHOSE IDEA WAS THIS 'BRING-YOUR-CONFOUNDED-PET-TO-WORK' DAY?"

Where are those nice blue fish that we like — the ones with the green stripes?
WE ATE THEM ALL — THEY'RE NOW EXTINCT.
S. harris

"FIRST, WOOL. THEN, LAMB CHOPS. NOW THEY'VE GOT US CREATING ANTIBIOTICS FOR THEM."

"YOU OUGHT TO WISE UP, AND GET INTO A MORE CONTEMPORARY LIFESTYLE — AND THE FIRST STEP IS TO BECOME A VEGETARIAN."

CAT WITH ALL THE
HAIR HE HAS EVER SHED

s.harris

He may be old and shaggy, but he gets me there and brings me back.

"THE LIONS LEAVE IT OVER — WE EAT IT. THE LEOPARDS DON'T LIKE IT — WE EAT IT. IF THAT'S NOT AN EATING DISORDER, WHAT IS?"

"THAT MAY BE YOUR DESCRIPTION, BUT WE DON'T THINK OF IT AS TERRORIZING THE NEIGHBORHOOD."

"BUT MOUNTAIN GOATS NEVER GET ACROPHOBIA."

"YOU SHOULD HAVE SEEN HOW EXCITED I MADE A COUPLE OF OCEANOGRAPHERS TODAY."

"I'VE BEEN TAGGED BY A WHALING COMMISSION, SOME ENVIRONMENT PEOPLE, A NAVAL RESEARCH TEAM, A FISHING GROUP, SOME ZOOLOGISTS..."

"HEY— NICE PLACE!"

"WE'RE A PROTECTED SPECIES AND AN ENDANGERED SPECIES, BUT WHEN I SEE A PERSON, I DON'T KNOW IF HE'S PROTECTING US OR ENDANGERING US."

"TALKING TO YOU IS FUTILE. I'M BEGINNING TO REGRET I EVER ESCAPED FROM THE PRIMATE SPEECH INSTITUTE."

They've been gone for hours, and it looks like they're not coming back. The first thing I have to figure out is how to pay the rent.
S.Harris

"THEY GET ALONG BEAUTIFULLY. THE DOG THINKS HE'S A CAT, AND THE CAT THINKS SHE'S A DOG."

"I HAVE NO IDEA WHAT SHOES AND POCKETBOOKS ARE, BUT THOSE WORDS GIVE ME THE WILLIES."

Why do they call us pests?
We bite them.
We eat their food.
We give them the willies, and that's all there is to it.
S. harris

They worry about **their** cholesterol, but they don't give a **damn** about ours!
S. Harris

"WE PECK AT GRAVEL, WE PECK AT STICKS, WE PECK AT THE GROUND...LIFE IS FULL OF DISAPPOINTMENTS."

"YOU SHOULDN'T WORRY. ASIDE FROM THE DUCK BILL AND THE EGGS, YOU'RE A PERFECTLY NORMAL MAMMAL."

THE ANIMAL RESEARCHER REPORTS...
I'VE BEEN WATCHING THIS HERD OF CATTLE FOR SEVEN YEARS, AND, TO BE FRANK, I HAVEN'T SEEN THEM DO ANYTHING YET!
S. Harris

LEONARDO DA VINCI'S CAT

S. Harris

"SOME OF THOSE YOUNGSTERS HAVE COME UP WITH A TERRIFIC NEW IDEA— FEATHERS."

I USE THE USUAL TRIPOD GAIT— FRONT AND BACK LEGS ON ONE SIDE ALONG WITH THE MIDDLE LEG ON THE OTHER SIDE.
I NEVER EVEN THOUGHT ABOUT IT. I JUST MOVE LOTS OF LEGS, AND THEN I MOVE LOTS OF OTHER LEGS.
S. Harris

RETIRED ELEPHANTS LIVING WITH THEIR MEMORIES — THEIR LONG, DETAILED, COMPLETE, ENDLESS MEMORIES

"BAD NEWS, MUFFY— YOU'RE BEING DISQUALIFIED ON A TECHNICALITY."

"I TOLD HIM WE'RE BECOMING AN ENDANGERED SPECIES. HE JUST LAUGHED."

MAN'S BEST
FRIEND

MAN'S WORST
FRIEND

MAN'S ONLY
FRIEND

Your feet can hurt, or you can have a headache. When you're a cephalopod, that's about it.
S. Harris

DOCUMENTARY PROOF: A DOG LOST HUNDREDS OF FEET FROM HOME CAN EASILY FIND HIS WAY BACK